For my dear parents.
Bola & Dayo.

WHAT IS A VOLCANO?

Imagine a big mountain that can sometimes go
BOOM! and SPLASH! like a giant bottle of soda when
you shake it too much. Well. that's a Volcano!
But instead of soda. it throws
out hot melted rocks and ash
into the sky.

WHAT MAKES A VOLCANO SO INTERESTING?

FIRE AND LAVA

Volcanoes spit up a river of liquid fire called Lava. it's a super-hot. glowing orange goo that flows out of the Earth surface.

MAGMA

Deep below the Earth's surface. it is so hot that some rocks slowly melt and become a thick flowing substance called Magma. When there are cracks large enough for it to escape. magma will make its way to the surface.

It travels up. up. up through the volcano and bursts out in a fiery explosion! That's an eruption!

MAGMA VS. LAVA

Magma is what we call the hot, gooey stuff deep inside the Earth, but when it comes out and flows on the surface, we call it lava.

EARTHQUAKE

An earthquake happens when the ground shakes because of the moving pieces called TECTONIC PLATES, beneath the Earth's surface. Volcanoes can make the ground shake and go BOOM!

→ Lava

→ Magma

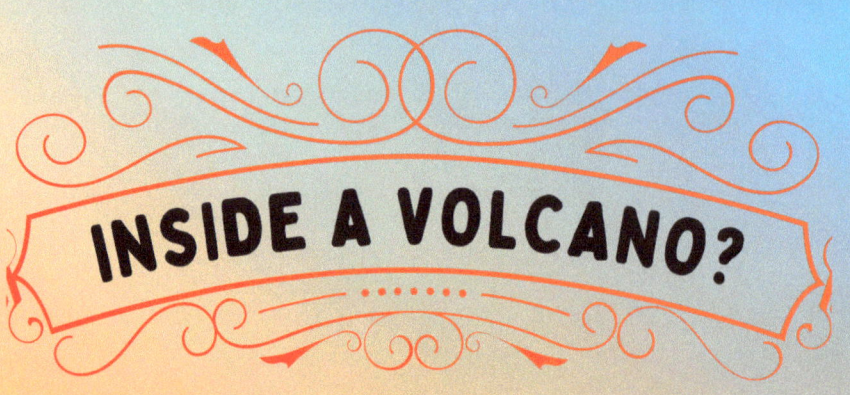

INSIDE A VOLCANO?

Let's take a peek inside a volcano.

+

+

GASES

Imagine you have a bottle of soda. When you shake it. there are bubbles. right? Well. inside the Earth. there are gases. a bit like those bubbles.

MAGMA

These gases hang out with Magma. the hot melted rock deep inside the belly of the volcano. creating a big. bubbly mix.

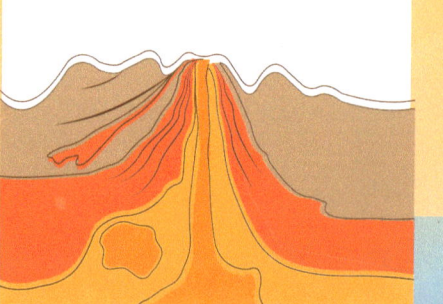

PRESSURE

As more and more magma and gas gather inside the volcano. they want to burst out. This makes a lot of pressure build up. like a balloon getting ready to pop!

And then. when the pressure is just too much. BOOM!
The volcano erupts. and all that magma and gas burst out. making
a spectacular show in the sky.

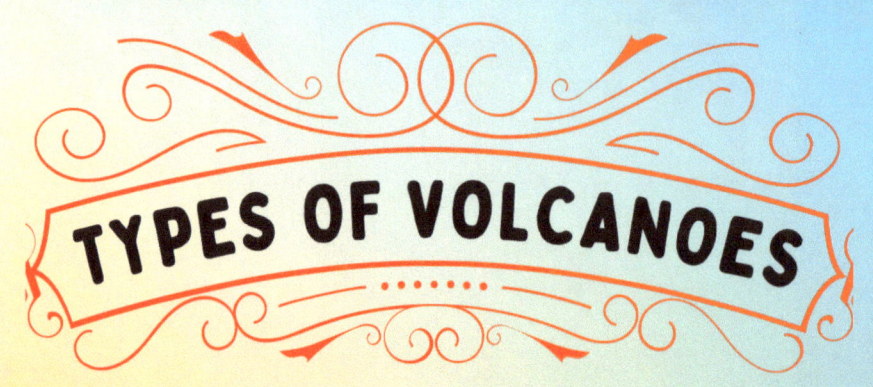

TYPES OF VOLCANOES

In this chapter, get ready to explore three amazing types of volcanoes. All three are like energetic mountains that shape the lands around them, but each has its own special way of showing off its unique personality!

SHIELD VOLCANO

Shield volcanoes are wide and not too steep. They are the largest volcanoes and often put on fiery shows. The lava from these giants flows lazily, and look like slow, gooey rivers.

Mauna Loa in Hawaii is the king of shield volcanoes. It's so big, you might need a telescope to see the top!

CINDER CONE

Cinder cones are the simplest and most common type of volcano. The lava from cinder cones is not flowy, it shoots out of the ground, falls around the opening and then cools to form the cone shape.

Paricutin in Mexico is a cool cinder cone. It decided to pop up in a farmer's field one day — talk about being full of surprises!

STRATOVOLCANO

Stratovolcanoes are tall mountains with a cone shape made from many layers of hard lava. When they erupt, they spit out thick lava and rocks that don't flow easily. This makes the eruption build up around the top, creating steep sides.

Mount Fuji in Japan is a famous stratovolcano. It's so famous, you might spot it on postcards and in cartoons!

Cinder cones are like the popcorn of volcanoes, quick and poppy! They shoot up high in the sky, and cool quickly.

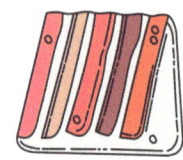

Picture a huge, towering mountain with layers like a delicious cake – that's a stratovolcano. They're like the rockstars of volcanoes!

Imagine a giant turtle shell on the ground – that's a shield volcano. It's wide and not too steep.

CINDER CONE

STRATOVOLCANO

SHIELD VOLCANO

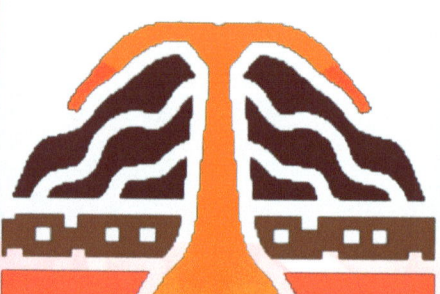

So, we have shield volcanoes that are wide and gentle, stratovolcanoes that are tall and explosive, and cinder cones that are small and quick.

But guess what? There are even more types of volcanoes out there, each with its own special way of surprising us. We'll keep our explorer hats on for future journeys and discover even more exciting volcanoes in the world!

ERUPTIONS

Did you know that not all volcanoes erupt?
There are ACTIVE volcanoes that are wide awake
and can erupt at any time.
The other kind of volcanoes are known as DORMANT.
These are like sleepy volcanoes. They've taken a break from
erupting, but who knows?
They might wake up and throw a lava
surprise someday!

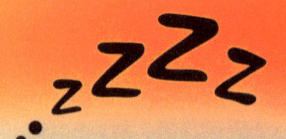

And then we have the EXTINCT volcanoes, which are like the
sleepyheads of the volcano family — they've snoozed for so
long that they're not expected to erupt again!

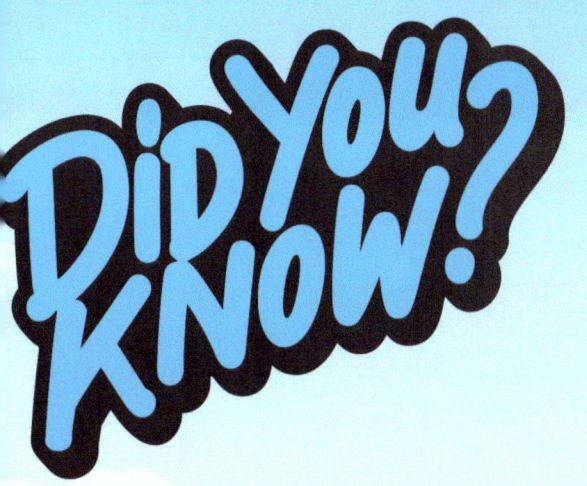

Did You Know?

The lava from some volcanoes can be so hot that it glows in different colors!

1500

Did you know there are about One thousand five hundred active volcanoes on Earth? That's a lot!

MARS

It's not just Earth that has volcanoes. Mars has the biggest volcano in our solar system called Olympus Mons.

Not all volcanoes are on land. Many are hidden beneath the ocean's surface, and when they erupt, they can create new islands!

Long ago, in Italy, a city called Pompeii got frozen in time when a big volcano named Mount Vesuvius erupted.

COMMON STAGES OF ERUPTION

COOLING DOWN

After the eruption. things start to cool down. Lava hardens. and the volcano goes back to a quiet state.

SHOWTIME

The volcano erupts! Lava flows. ash clouds fill the sky. and sometimes. there are loud explosions.

GETTING READY

Magma. which is the hot. melted rock inside the Earth. starts moving upward toward the surface. Pressure builds up inside the volcano.

WAKE-UP CALL

The volcano shows it might wake up soon with signs like earthquakes. rising steam or swelling ground.

QUIET AND CALM

The volcano seems to be asleep. with no signs of activity. This is the quiet time. and it's called the dormant stage.

Remember. not all volcanoes follow these steps exactly. and some might skip stages or have differences. Nature loves to surprise us!

ERUPTION VOCABULARY

PYROCLASTIC FLOW

Think of a super-fast river made of hot rocks and gas rushing down the mountain. That's a pyroclastic flow!

FIREWORKS

Sometimes, there are fireworks too, as rocks burst out, making the eruption even more amazing.

ASH CLOUDS

When a volcano erupts, it can send up a cloud made of tiny bits of rock and hot air — that's the ash cloud.

LAVA

When Magma travels up and reaches the top, it becomes lava, flowing down the sides of the volcano.

MAGMA

Remember Magma, the super-hot, melted rocks deep inside the belly of volcanoes?

START

FAMOUS VOLCANOES

Get ready for an exciting volcano celebrity
show in this chapter!
We'll explore seven of the coolest volcanoes
around the world. These special volcanoes make
new land. keep stories from the past. and turn
into amazing places for climbing and hiking.

They all have incredible tales about
shaping the Earth.

Take a close look at the pictures in the next
pages and see if you can guess if they're cinder
cones. shield. or stratovolcanoes.

YELLOWSTONE (NORTH AMERICA)

Yellowstone is a park of wonders with a super-volcano under it!
Picture a volcano so huge it could hold many others. Yellowstone's last big
eruption was 640.000 years ago — that's a really. really long time ago! Scientists
keep an eye on it. but don't worry. it's not planning to erupt anytime soon.

MOUNT VESUVIUS (ITALY)

Vesuvius is the history keeper in Italy. Long ago. it erupted and buried the city of Pompeii under lots of ash. People in Pompeii were caught off guard. frozen in time. The city was found much later. and now it's like a time machine. showing us how people lived back then.

MOUNT KILIMANJARO (TANZANIA)

Did you know Tanzania has an amazing volcano called Mount Kilimanjaro?
It's a huge stratovolcano that looks like it's wearing a cap of snow and ice.
Kilimanjaro last erupted a whopping 360.000 years ago! It is the tallest mountain
in Africa. and many people love to visit and climb it for a thrilling adventure.

MOUNT FUJI (JAPAN)

Mount Fuji is a big deal because it's a symbol of Japan. The last time it erupted was way before most of us were born, making it a calm and peaceful mountain that people love to admire, climb, and even tell stories about.

EYJAFJALLAJÖKULL (ICELAND)

Eyjafjallajökull is a tongue-twisting volcano in Iceland. When it erupted in 2010, it sent a lot of ash into the sky, making it difficult for planes to fly in Europe. This event showed us that even faraway volcanoes can have a big impact on our world.

MAUNA LOA (HAWAII)

Mauna Loa. the big. friendly volcano in Hawaii. has a long history of lava adventures. It's so huge that if you stand at the bottom and look up. it feels like you're looking at the sky! Because it's so big and close to people. scientists always watch it carefully to make sure everyone stays safe.

MOUNT ST. HELENS (UNITED STATES)

Mount St. Helens is an active volcano in the United States. In 1980, it had a big eruption that changed the land around it. Before the big explosion, Mount St. Helens had lots of shaking and steam coming out for two months. Then, there was a huge fiery blast that spread ash in eleven U.S. states and parts of Canada!

VOLCANIC TREASURES

Have you ever wondered about the different types of fascinating rocks formed during volcanic eruptions?

Well, get ready to dive in and ask yourself – which of these rocks have you seen or heard of before?

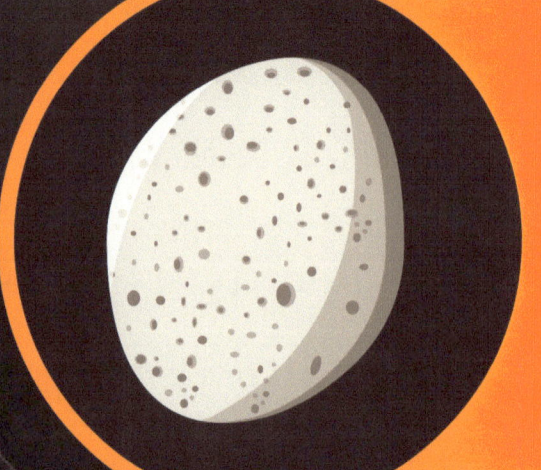

PUMICE

Imagine a rock so light it can float! That's pumice, created when frothy lava cools quickly. Its bubbly texture makes it perfect for scrubbing and cleaning.

OBSIDIAN

Meet obsidian. the rock that's as smooth and shiny as glass is formed when lava cools very quickly. Ancient people used obsidian to make sharp tools and arrowheads.

CAN YOU GUESS OTHER WAYS THE ROCKS ARE USED?

* _____
* _____
* _____
* _____

GRANITE

Granite shows up a long time after a volcano erupts. It's strong and shiny. with little pieces of different minerals mixed into its designs.

LIVING NEAR VOLCANOES

Imagine living in a place like no other – a volcano!
Picture dealing with scorching heat, shaky ground,
and air so tough it can make your head spin!
In this super harsh environment, where everything,
even the water and air, can be poisonous, there are special animals
that call it home.

POMPEII WORM

Meet the incredible Pompeii Worm, a true champ in hot deep sea. This worm can handle super, super hot places (even hotter than boiling water!), and it makes its home right by these very hot spots. The Pompeii Worm is a real tough guy, for sure!

VAMPIRE GROUND FINCH

The Vampire Ground Finch may sound spooky, but it's only after blood for the nutrients it needs to survive when seeds and insects are scarce. This clever bird has a special beak like a tool, allowing it to feed on the blood of seabirds. It's an unusual but smart way to survive.

LESSER FLAMINGO

The water in Lake Natron gets really, really hot! It's also full of minerals that can be harmful for plants, animals, and people. But for Lesser flamingos, their tough skin and leg scales protect them from getting burned. Plus, they can drink super-hot water and filter out salt using their special noses.

FEMALE LAND IGUANAS

Female land iguanas on the Galapagos Islands lay their eggs in the warm volcanic ash, creating a cozy nursery. This smart choice acts like a natural incubator, keeping the eggs warm and safe until they're ready to hatch.

HOT AND HAPPY PLANTS

Plants can survive in challenging volcano areas too! Let's explore four awesome examples that love growing in the rocky, hot places created by volcanoes.

SILVERSWORD

Meet the Haleakalā Silversword! It's a tough plant with shiny hairs and thick leaves that can survive in hot, dry places like the Haleakalā volcano. These plants live for 3 to 90 years, bloom once in a spectacular way, make seeds, and then spread them in the wind.

OHIA LEHUA

This tree is from Hawaii, and it's special because it has bright red flowers. You can usually find it on volcanoes, and it's one of the first plants to grow on new lava.

LAVA PHLOX

This tough plant has bright pink or purple flowers and grows in soil from volcanoes.

RED HOT POKER (TORCH LILY)

Meet the Torch Lily! This plant has tall spikes of tube-shaped flowers in red, orange, and yellow colors. It's cool because it can grow in soil from volcanoes.

Did you notice that many plants near volcanoes have bright colors? It's not by chance - these colors help them attract helpful insects that help them grow new seeds.

VOLCANIC SAFETY

Did you know? Some cultures think volcanoes are sacred and have powerful gods inside. People treat them with lots of respect. and that's one reason why locals stay near these amazing mountains.

But that's not all. The soil around volcanoes is like magic for farmers – it's really good for growing food.

It's really, really beautiful around volcanoes.
The rocks, mountains, and even hot springs make these
places look amazing.

Imagine climbing and hiking around a volcano!
It's a playground for
people who love adventures.

STAYING SAFE AROUND VOLCANOES

Living near volcanoes can be exciting, but it's super important for people to know about the possible dangers and be ready.
Communities in these areas usually have safety plans and ways to leave quickly if there's a chance of a volcano erupting.

They pay close attention to warnings from experts and local authorities. If there's a chance of an eruption, they know what to do.

Families and communities create plans for what to do if a volcano erupts. This includes knowing where to go, how to get there, and what to bring.

They practice what to do in case of an emergency. Just like fire drills at school, they have volcano drills to make sure everyone knows how to stay safe.

People keep emergency kits ready with things like water, food, first aid supplies, and important documents.

If there's a real danger, they leave their homes quickly and go to a safe place. This helps them stay out of harm's way.

They use masks and goggles to shield themselves from ash and debris during an eruption.

Volcanic eruptions are like nature's wild show – a natural disaster that can cause serious damage and affect lives.

But here's the cool part- they also have this superpower to make things new, where people, plants, and animals do really well.

TEST YOUR VOLCANO KNOWLEDGE

QUIZ TIME

1 What is magma, and where does it come from?

2 What happens during a volcanic eruption?

3 Describe shield volcanoes and how their lava flows.

4 What is an extinct volcano?

5 What are some signs that a volcano might erupt soon?

6 Name two famous volcanoes mentioned in the book and share an interesting fact about each.

8 Name one type of rock formed by volcanoes

7 Why do some people choose to live near volcanoes?

9 Why is the Lesser Flamingo able to survive in the hot water of Lake Natron?

FIND THE WORDS!

VOLCANO, LAVA, MAGMA, ERUPTION, SHIELD, STRATOVOLCANO,
DORMANT, ACTIVE, EARTHQUAKE, MOUNTAIN, EARTH, PUMICE, GRANITE, OBSIDIAN, FLOWER

E	D	D	U	V	R	Y	Z	U	S	Q	D	H	O	O
G	N	N	W	R	B	S	G	W	A	C	T	I	V	E
P	S	T	R	A	T	O	V	O	L	C	A	N	O	Q
U	U	D	H	M	E	U	O	G	I	F	L	O	W	E	R
M	I	Q	R	Q	H	H	H	T	V	S	R	E	R	W
I	E	A	R	T	H	Q	U	A	K	E	R	A	F	V
C	U	E	M	G	W	M	O	V	G	C	Q	R	W	D
E	T	B	W	P	D	O	B	O	Y	G	Z	T	E	O
S	H	I	E	L	D	U	S	L	J	R	P	H	R	R
T	Y	L	S	R	U	N	I	C	H	A	B	U	U	M
U	M	A	Q	V	M	T	D	A	R	N	Q	Z	P	A
T	C	V	F	X	A	A	I	N	Q	I	A	H	T	N
G	C	A	M	E	G	I	A	O	P	T	X	O	I	T
C	K	U	Z	U	M	N	N	W	X	E	Y	U	O	H
C	J	D	S	Z	A	Z	A	P	U	W	Y	M	N	J

SCIENCE

Did you know you could create your own mini volcano and make it erupt with fizzing lava? Grab your safety goggles and get ready to be a volcanic wizard in 3. 2. 1....

WHAT YOU WILL NEED

- Plastic bottle
- Baking soda
- Dish soap
- Vinegar
- Playdough or Clay
- Red food coloring
- Tray

1. Place the plastic bottle on the tray to contain the mess.
2. Create a mountain shape using playdough or modeling clay around the small plastic bottle. leaving the top open.
3. Add a teaspoon of baking soda into the bottle.
4. Mix a few drops of dish soap with red food coloring and pour it into the bottle.
5. When ready for eruption. pour vinegar into the bottle. and watch the volcanic eruption!

WORD SEARCH SOLUTION

VOLCANO, LAVA, MAGMA, ERUPTION, SHIELD, STRATOVOLCANO,
DORMANT, ACTIVE, EARTHQUAKE, MOUNTAIN, EARTH, PUMICE, GRANITE, OBSIDIAN, FLOWER

E	D	D	U	V	R	Y	Z	U	S	Q	D	H	O	O
G	N	N	W	R	B	S	G	W	A	C	T	I	V	E
P	S	T	R	A	T	O	V	O	L	C	A	N	O	Q
U	D	H	M	E	U	O	G	I	F	L	O	W	E	R
M	I	Q	R	Q	H	H	H	T	V	S	R	E	R	W
I	E	A	R	T	H	Q	U	A	K	E	R	A	F	V
C	U	E	M	G	W	M	O	V	G	C	Q	R	W	D
E	T	B	W	P	D	O	B	O	Y	G	Z	T	E	O
S	H	I	E	L	D	U	S	L	J	R	P	H	R	R
T	Y	L	S	R	U	N	I	C	H	A	B	U	U	M
U	M	A	Q	V	M	T	D	A	R	N	Q	Z	P	A
T	C	V	F	X	A	A	I	N	Q	I	A	H	T	N
G	C	A	M	E	G	I	A	O	P	T	X	O	I	T
C	K	U	Z	U	M	N	N	W	X	E	Y	U	O	H
C	J	D	S	Z	A	Z	A	P	U	W	Y	M	N	J

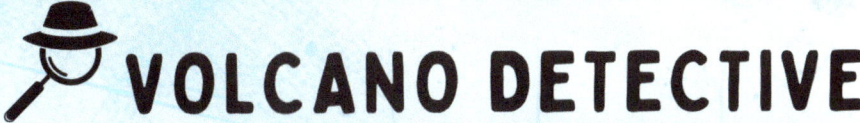

VOLCANO DETECTIVE

These stratovolcanoes sure know how to steal the volcanic spotlight!

Mount Vesuvius is a stratovolcano.

Mount Kilimanjaro is a stratovolcano.

Mount Fuji is a stratovolcano.

Eyjafjallajökull is a stratovolcano

Mauna Loa is a shield volcano.

Mount St. Helens is a stratovolcano.

Nature is full of surprises, and volcanoes are just the beginning. Keep exploring to find out more about the secrets that make our planet super special!

SCAN HERE

Share Your Thoughts on this Book!
Your opinion is incredibly valuable to me, and I would be
thrilled if you could leave a review.
Also, don't forget to scan the QR code above to stay
connected for more exciting content and updates!